Rhymes And Reasons

- a poetic approach to mathematical concepts

anupama singh

Made with ❤ on the BookLeaf Publishing Platform
www.bookleafpub.in
www.bookleafpub.com

Dedication

To all children who struggle with math , like I did - May this book be your guiding light to math mastery.

To my family - my constant source of love and support.

And to my dear father , who left us too soon , but is remembered each day. Thank you for being my guiding light.

Preface

Why I wrote this book ?

This book was born out of a pressing need : to help children struggling with mathematics understand and enjoy the subject. Having worked with children for 28 years, I have continually looked for ways to simplify complex concepts. Over time I started crafting stories and poems to make learning math a delightful experience.

The poems in this book are meant to be read for pleasure, and need not be memorized. Just by reading these poems ,the students will develop a deeper understanding of mathematical concepts .

Math is a vast and intricate subject, with numerous concepts to grasp. In this book I have focused on the essential ideas that bridge the gap between basic counting and higher level Math, providing a solid foundation to young generation to flourish.

I am confident that this book will be a valuable resource for students, parents and educators seeking to make mathematics more engaging and accessible. Thank you for joining me on this journey to make math fun and exciting for all.

Acknowledgements

Writing this book would not have been possible without the love, support and encouragement of my family and friends.

I want to thank a few people in particular:

My husband , for his unwavering patience and understanding when I needed it the most.

My children, Ashutosh, Sheetal , Aparna , my friend Purnima, for reviewing the poems for conceptual errors .

My son, Abhishek for guiding me in writing the preface.

My mother, sisters-in -law Geeta Singh and Muntaha , and brothers Shailendra and Farhat for believing in me.

And to all my other family members, friends and colleagues, who have been a constant source of inspiration and motivation.

I am forever grateful.

1. The zero trail

In the realm of numbers, a trail is laid.
with zero at its heart , a path is made.
let's take this journey, a wondrous spin.
zero leads the way, revealing math's secret within.

A symbol of nothing , where a secret lies.
It multiplies values, with mighty surprise.
From ones to tens , it's a wondrous ride.
Add a zero, and ten times you'll glide.

A hundred has, two zeros in a tow,
with each added zero, the count grow.
A thousand has three , ten thousands four.
Add 5 to get a lakh, for ten thousands add one more.

A crore's grandeur with 7 zeros aligned.
Ten crores splendor, with 8 zeros find.
So let's cherish zero, for all its might.
A tiny digit , that shines with delight.

2. KISME KITNE ZERO

आओ बच्चों तुम्हे सिखाएं INDIAN NUMERATION.
बहुत है easy ,बहुत आसान, मत लो कोई tension.

अरे! देखो ! यह आया number 1 हमारा hero.
इसके आगे लगा के देखें हम अनेको zero.

one zero -tens
2 zeros-hundreds

3 zeros-thousands
4 zeros- ten thousands
5 zeros- lakhs
6 zeros-ten lakhs

7 zeros- crores
8 zeros- ten crores

देखा तुमको नहीं रहा अब कोई confusion .
कितनी जल्दी समझ आ गया INDIAN NUMERATION.

3. Face value

In numerals, a secret lies
A value that meets the eye.
Face value , a simple name
The digit's worth , in its own frame.

Come and see
how I look!
The face value of a digit is
how you see me in your nursery book.

Like six is a number,
simple and plain.
Face value - just 6 ,
no need to explain.

Still confused ?
You need advise?
Take out a pencil
And just write.

Write one , nine , and seven
Now two , three , five and eight.
You have just written the face values
of all the digits , isn't that great.!

4. 54327619-what's this !

ध्यान से देखो इन 8 digits को, और बताओ हमको I
कैसे लिखे इसे कि, सब पढ़ पाएं इस नंबर को I

पढ़ना आएगा सबको , और पता चलेगी वैल्यू I
सिस्टम इंटरनेशनल या इंडियन , दे दो कोई cue.

दोनों मे ही क्यों ना , करे इसे हम try.
comma का है खेल ये सारा , Why this hue n cry ?

कॉमा के संग नामो मे भी, कुछ फर्क है होता I
याद रख पाएं जो इनको, उनका कुछ नहीं खोता I

Hundred thousands एक लाख है , ten lakhs एक million.
ten millions एक crore बन जाता, 100 crores एक billion.

आओ ,अब हम करें ,कॉमा को प्लेस I
three digits right से , पहले कॉमा का है space.
फिर Indian में two डिजिट्स पर ,इंटरनेशनल में three,
Periods के नाम याद कर , पढ़ लो नंबर free.

5. Place value

I am a digit
with a face.
but my value changes ,
with change in place.

Relocating my place in a number
changes my worth.
I can be 7 hundred or crore
though I am just 7 by birth.

The ones place is where
my place and face value is same.
Then it grows ten times
as I move to the left in frame.

Ones ,tens .hundreds ,thousands,
lakhs and crore.
Hope you have understood
or do you want more ?

So when you are reading numbers
don't be slow.
Remember place values, and let
your knowledge grow.

6. Number five increased its value

आओ सुनाएँ तुम्हें इक कहानी I
इसमें न कोई राजा ,न है कोई रानी I

कहानी है Number 5 की ,सोचे, कैसे अपनी वैल्यू बढ़ाऊँ ?
कैसे Number 6,7,8 और 9 से आगे बढ़ जाऊँ ?

तो सोच रहा है , क्या है इसका SOLUTION .
Face तो change होता नहीं , क्या change करूँ POSITION?

तो चल पड़ा RIGHT से LEFT , Change करने POSITION.
Ones से tens फिर hundreds, thousands , हो गया VALUE CREATION.

5 हो गया arrogant ,पा कर इतनी RECOGNITION.
भूल गया गिरेगी Value , Left to Right RELOCATION.

तो समझे ! FACE VALUE वही रहती है , मत लो कोई TENSION.
PLACE VALUE change करनी हो तो , change करो
POSITION.

7. Measuring length, mass and capacity.

In Math , we measure with precision so fine.
Length, mass, and capacity, all in line.

Meters, centimeters. millimeters and kilometers too.
units of Length, to measure anew.

1000 mm make a meter so bright,
1000 meters make a km, a longer sight.

For mass use grams and kilograms with care,
1 kilogram equals 1000 grams, a weight to share.

For capacity, use milliliters and liters so fine,
1 liter equals 1000 milliliters, a volume divine.

Measuring with accuracy, in Math we take pride,
Length, mass ,and capacity, side by side.

8. III,11,3, ३ -NUMBERS OR NUMERALS

Draw three downstrokes , tall and calm.
Followed by two , with an arm.

Then two curves , a wavy delight.
Facing left , at times with a tail tight.

You can guess the symbols in sight.
If you could draw them perfectly right.

Did you just shout with glee,
that those are nothing but number three.

III , three lines so bold.
Roman numbers , stories untold.

3, a digit so sleek.
Arabic number, precision unique.

11, two lines so fine.
binary number system , developed with time.

३ , in the script Devanagari
looks unique, all would agree.

They all are NUMERALS
of system distinct.

To represent NUMBER 3.
is the same intent.

9. EVEN OR ODD

Take a handful of eclairs
and put in pairs of two , to mingle.
Did each one find a partner
or one is left , alone and single ?

If each one found a partner
with a none left over.
You paired them EVEN
As on each other they hover .

If one could not be paired
and was left alone. Oh, God!
Your handful of eclairs
was numbered in ODD.

EVEN or ODD
a number's fate,
is decided by 2
their dividing state.

Divide a number by 2
And you get a zero.
The number is EVEN,
Yet he is no hero.

Divide a number by 2
And you get 1,
The number is ODD
But the problem is none.

10. PRIME OR COMPOSITE

Prime and Composite
Opposites in might,
Are positive integers,
defined by divisors , in sight.

If a number can't be divided
except by 1 and itself too.
Then it's PRIME,
with factors only two.

There are numbers with more
than two factors in sight.
We call them COMPOSITE
important, shining bright.

2, the EVEN PRIME ,stands
alone in its place.
All other EVEN numbers
are COMPOSITE , with a different face.

Among, ODD NUMBERS , some are
PRIME , unique and rare.
While others are COMPOSITE, with
factors to share.

11. ray, line and line segment

In geometry's realm,
we find our way,
with Rays, Lines , and line segments,
night and day.

A ray extends , infinitely far and
wide.
From a single point , it glides with
pride.

A line, a path, that stretches, long
and true,
Extends in both directions, for me
and you.

A line segment , bounded, with ends
in sight,
Connects two points , a finite,
shining light.

These geometric friends, help us
explore,
The world of shapes, and Math,
evermore.

12. Roman Numerals-a story unique

In days of old, in the Roman
Empire's might,
There was a village, numbered
1 in sight.
It was called I, a name that's stood
the test,
A village steeped in history , and
legends of the best.

Though it was village number one,
so grand and so fair,
It had only 50 Locals , with a love
without compare.
They adored their flurry friends,
with hearts so true and kind,
500 Dogs and 100 Cats, a pet
lover's paradise to find.

One day, disaster struck, the pets
fell ill and weak,
But fear not, for the village had
Vets to seek.
Though only 5 in number, they
worked with skill and care,
and with 1000 Machines beeping, and
10 X-rays to share.

The 50 LOCALS were grateful,
for the care so fine and true,
Their 100 CATS and 500 DOGS
recovered quickly, thanks to
5 VETS, 10 X-RAYS, AND
1000 MACHINES anew.

And now we know ,the Roman
numerals so fine.
I, V, X, L, C, D and M, a learning
journey divine.

13. factors and multiples

4*1=4
4*2=8
4*3=12
4*4=16

and so, we go as the number grow
but then take a pause,
for the cause-
to learn from the times tables,
what are factors and multiples.

4, 8,12 and 16,
are all multiples of 4.
Continue multiplying to get some more.
MULTIPLES are RESULTS of MULTIPLICATION,
see a few more to clear confusion.

Multiply 4 by 5, 6, 7, 8
and 9
20, 24, 28,

32, 36,
are all multiples of 4,
that shine.

But what are FACTORS,
you might wonder with zest?
FACTORS are the numbers
that DIVIDE
any number
WITH NO REST.

They are the numbers
that multiply
together to give you a score .
In this case , 4 is the factor of
4,8, 12,16,20
and more.

Try this
with other times tables,
to master
the concept of
factors and
multiples.

14. PRIME FACTORIZATION

To find PRIME FACTORS,
a task so fine.
Follow these steps,
and you'll shine.

Take a number,
any number will do.
And ask yourself,
'what factors are true?'

Start with 2,
the smallest PRIME of all.
If it divides evenly,
then you have a ball.

Keep dividing by 2,
until it won't go.
Then try by 3
and see if it will show.

Keep dividing by PRIME NUMBERS,
one by one.
Until you can't divide anymore,
you are done.

Write down the PRIME FACTORS
in the order you found.
And you'll have the PRIME FACTORIZATION,
spinning around.

For example, take 12,
a number so neat.
Its PRIME FACTORS are 2*2*3,
no one can beat.

Follow these steps,
and you'll be a pro.
In finding PRIME FACTORS,
isn't it, oh! bro!

15. LCM and HCF

Take multiples of two or more numbers in line.
Compare and find the smallest that shine.

The first common multiple you see ,
is the LEAST COMMON MULTIPLE , a Math decree.

Now, list the factors of each number.
find the common factor, don't slumber.

The greatest number that you see,
Is the HIGHEST COMMON FACTOR , all will agree.

Together they work, in harmony so true.
LCM and HCF ,a math duo.

16. Fractions- a simple explanation

A loaf of bread , no slices to share,
Five members at home , with hunger to spare.
Each wanted equal pieces, a fair request to make,
So I cut the bread into 10 pieces , for all to partake.

Two pieces for each, a fair and equal share.
2/10 for each, a FRACTION to show we care.
Simplified to 1/5, a part of the whole.
Each person got his share, me a happy soul.

A FRACTION is a piece of the whole, you see.
Represented as a/b, simple as can be.
A is the piece , the part that's shared.
B is the total, the pieces that are prepared.

Think of a pizza, cut into eight pieces so fine.
If you eat 4, your fraction is 4/8, all the time.
Or cut a cake into 12, with 3 pieces to eat.

Your fraction is 3/12, a tasty treat.

So remember, fractions are as easy as can be.
A piece of a whole, represented simply.

17. Fractions all around us

Why Fractions, you ask with a grin?
In cooking they help me measure within.
one quarter cup of sugar , just right.
Three - quarters teaspoon of salt, a delight.
To scale recipes up or down with ease,
I multiply or divide with expertise.

When shopping for deals , I am on the quest.
To find the best prices and pass the test.
'1/4 off' -buy 4 get 1 free
on a shirt that's just right for me.
comparing prices, fractions come into play,
Helping me shop smart, every single day.

My daily schedule's filled , with 1/3 work and play.
2/3 for rest and relaxation , at the end of the day.
Fractions in fitness, help me track my pace.
A 2/3 mile run , or a 1/4 mile sprint in its place.
In sports, fractions matter, in every single play.
A 3/4 court press, or a 1/2 court defense each day.

To create a soil blend just right.
For the container gardening site.
Mix 1/2 potting soil, as the base so fine.
With 1/4 compost, rich in nutrients divine.
Add 1/8 perlite, 1/8 coconut coir, too.
To retain water and see your plants through.

In music's rhythm, in art's proportion.
measurement precise , in the magic potion.
In mixing 1/2 red,1/4 of blue and yellow in a pint.
We get brown grey with a reddish tint..
Fractions everywhere, in life's every pace.
Helping us measure, create , and find our place.

18. Decimals- another kind of number.

Whole number stand alone so tall.
Fractions show parts, one and all.
But when they combine in a special way,
Decimals are born, come what may.

A mix of both, separated by a decimal point,
a dividing line.
to the left lies the whole,
to the right is the fractional sign.

3.57, has 3 as a whole
and .57 (57/100) a fraction, you see.
That's Decimal number,
for you and for me.

In science, finance and
cooking with flair,
Decimals play a crucial role
without compare.

In medicine, engineering,
interest rate, you see.
Decimals are essential,
for accuracy and clarity.

19. The Place value system in a decimal number

In the place value chart,
a pattern is found.
Moving left ,
the numbers increase, all around.

From ones to tens,
to hundreds, and more,
Each place value grows,
by ten times, evermore.

But what if we move,
to the other side?
From ones to tenths,
to hundredths, with pride.

The numbers decrease
by ten times, you see.
A reciprocal pattern,
for you and for me.

To the left of the ONES,
the TENS take their place.
But to the right ,
the TENTHS show their face.

The pattern continues,
with HUNDREDTHS and more.
Each place value shrinking,
by TEN times, evermore.

The places to the RIGHT,
of the decimal point,
Have "THS"
to their names, joint.

Tenths, hundredths,
thousandths, and more.
A decimal delight,
we all adore.

So now you know,
the secret of the chart.
A pattern of tens,
that's easy to start.

Moving left the decimal point ,
the numbers grow,
moving right they shrink.
A mathematical magic,
that's fun to think.

20. Angles--What and How

An angle is formed, where the two rays entwine.
The point where they meet is called the vertex so fine.

Angles come in various forms, you see.
Right, acute, obtuse, straight, reflex and complete.

Right angles, 90 degrees so fine.
Acute angles, less than 90, a sharp design.

Obtuse angles, greater than 90, a wide span,
Straight angles, 180 degrees, a straight line's plan.

Reflex angles, a range so wide,
Between 180 and 360, that reside.

A full rotation, a complete spin,
360 degrees, the circle within.

A protractor's semi-circle shape with two division.
Helps measure these angles with precision

Align the vertex with the midpoint zero mark,
And with the baseline too, to embark.

Then read the degrees, where the other ray crosses the scale,
that's the angle's measure, with no room to fail.

So, follow these steps, to measure with ease,
And find the angle's size, with expertise.

21. PERIMETER AND AREA

PERIMETER, a path so fine.
surrounds a shape. a BOUNDARY divine.

Add up the sides, one by one,
To find the distance, and you are done.

For rectangles, it's 2 (L+ b), a rule abide.
Squares , 4 multiplied by a side .

Triangle , add all three sides you see.
Circles, has circumference, for you and me.

AREA is the SPACE INSIDE A SHAPE that mattered ,
Rectangles, length into breadth ;Square, side squared .

Triangle, base into height divided by two , a formula grand .
Circles, just multiply Pi by the radius squared in hand.

Perimeter , walk on the sides , feel free.
Area is the measure of the inside space we see.

So calculate both with precision and care.
A path to perfection , beyond compare.

www.ingramcontent.com/pod-product-compliance
Lightning Source LLC
LaVergne TN
LVHW052105160826
845678LV00015B/3375